PIANO SOLO

CHRISTIAN CHRISTMAS FAVORITES

T0081852

ISBN-13: 978-1-4234-3160-2
ISBN-10: 1-4234-3160-X

HAL•LEONARD®
CORPORATION
7777 W. BLUEMOUND RD. P.O. BOX 13819 MILWAUKEE, WI 53213

Visit Hal Leonard Online at
www.halleonard.com

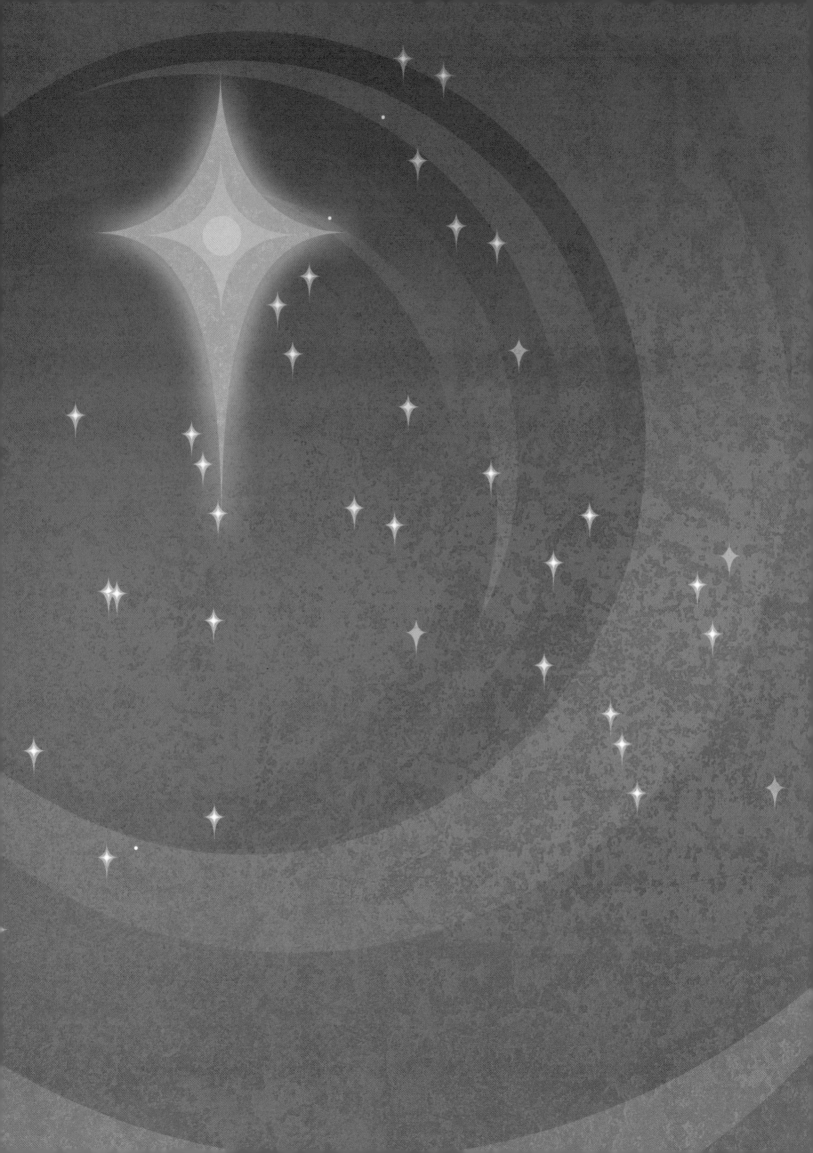

ALL IS WELL

Words and Music by MICHAEL W. SMITH
and WAYNE KIRKPATRICK

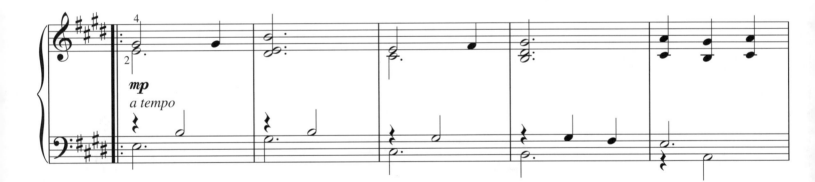

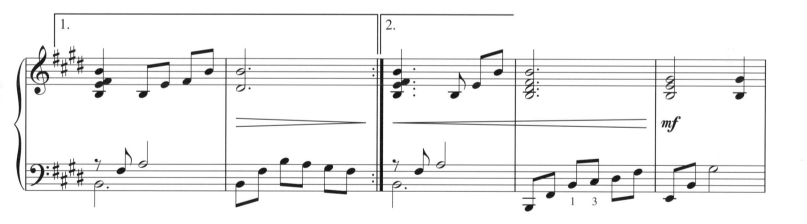

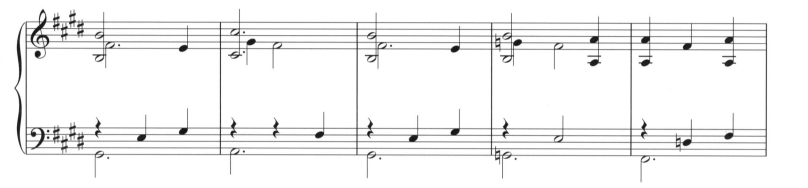

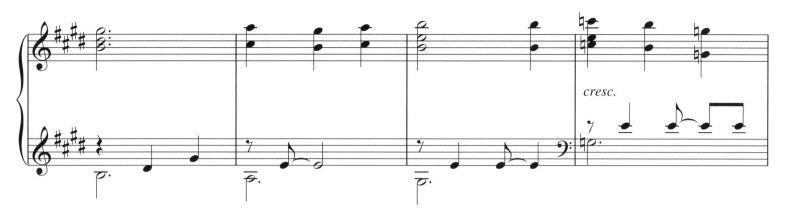

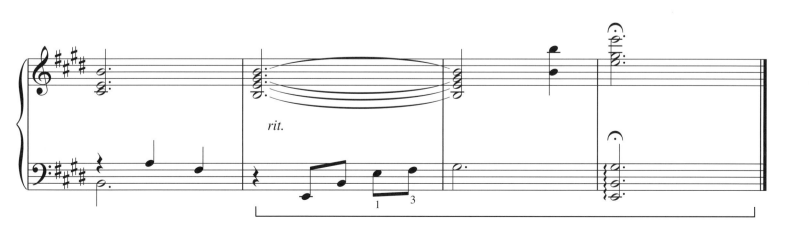

BREATH OF HEAVEN
(Mary's Song)

Words and Music by AMY GRANT
and CHRIS EATON

To Coda ⊕

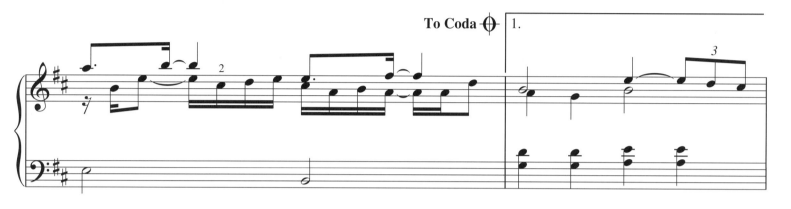

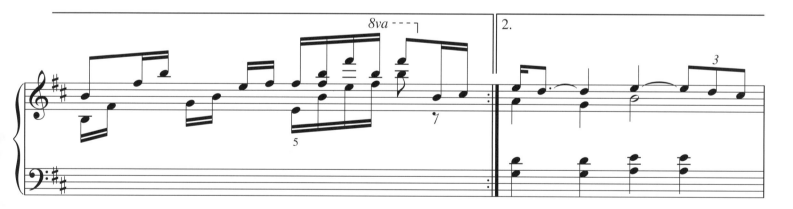

D.S. al Coda

CODA

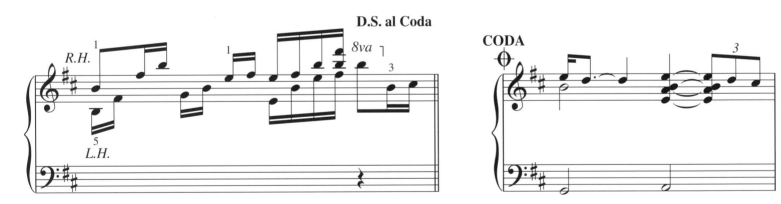

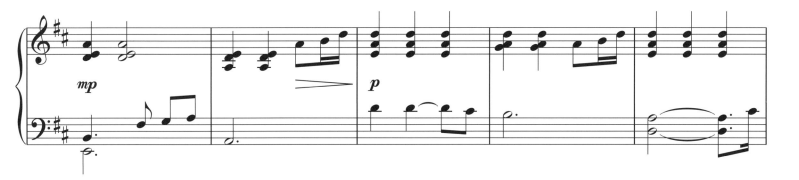

CHRISTMAS IS ALL IN THE HEART

Words and Music by
STEVEN CURTIS CHAPMAN

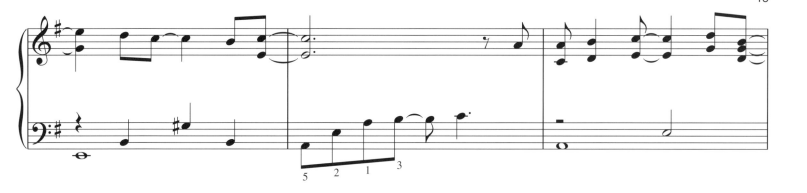

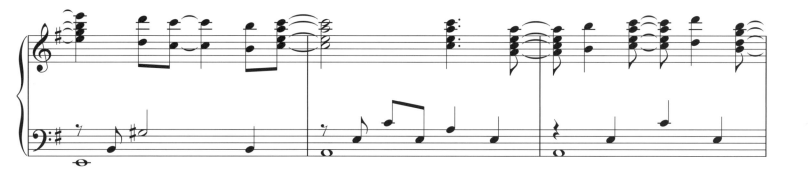

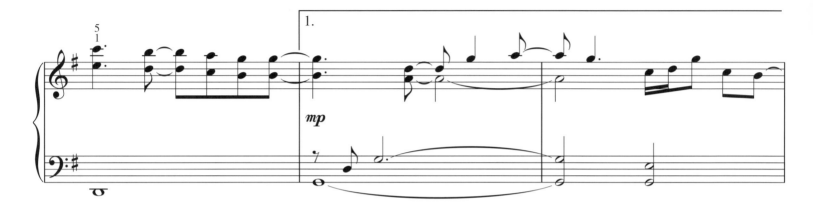

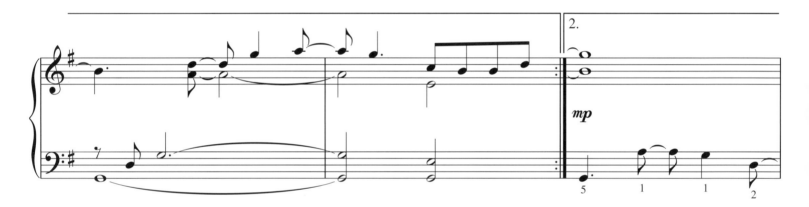

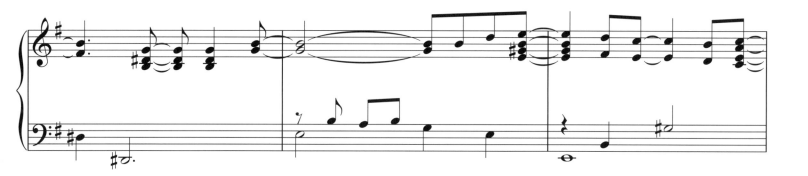

CHRISTMASTIME

Words and Music by MICHAEL W. SMITH
and JOANNA CARLSON

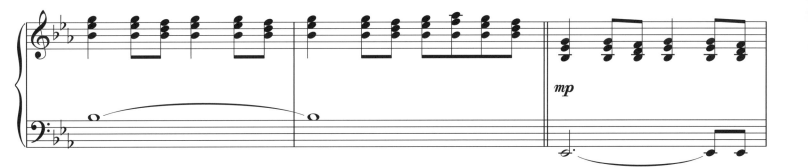

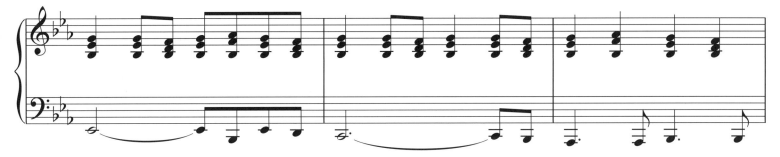

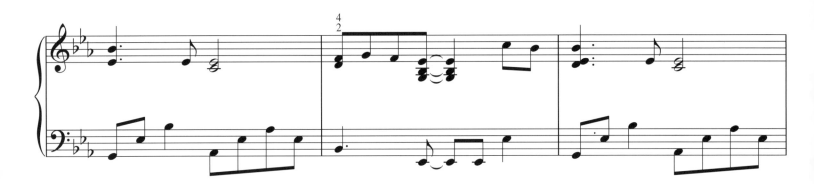

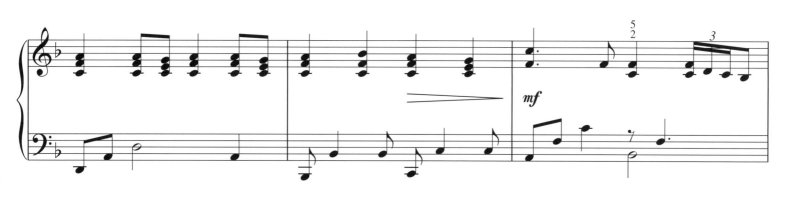

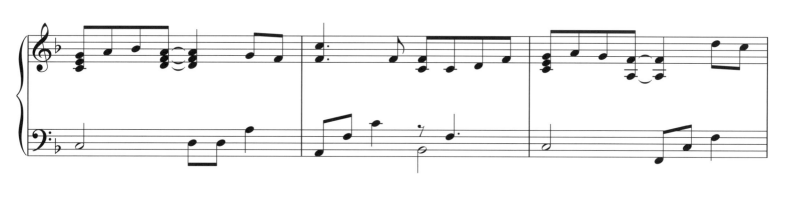

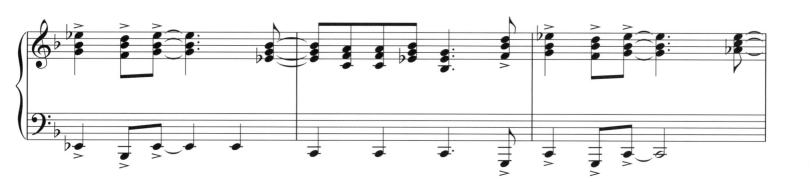

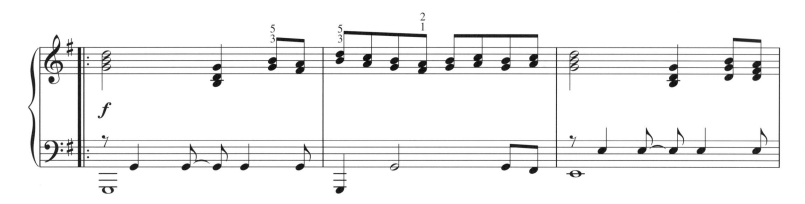

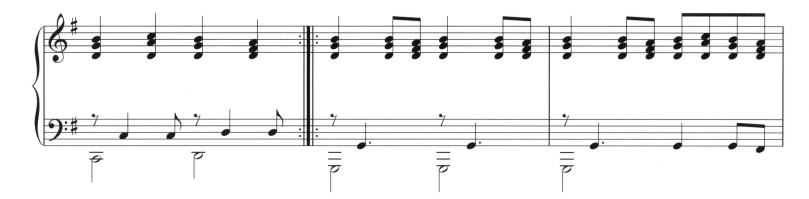

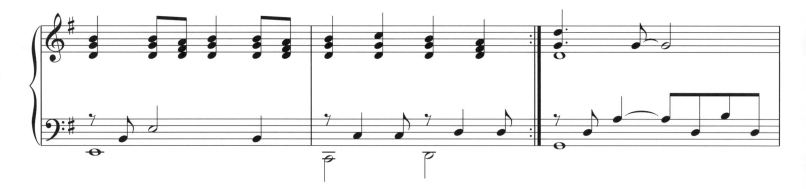

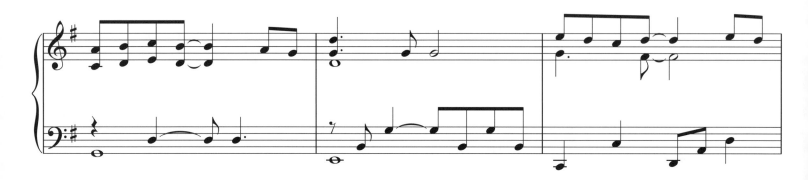

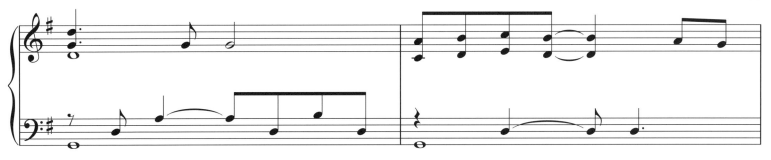

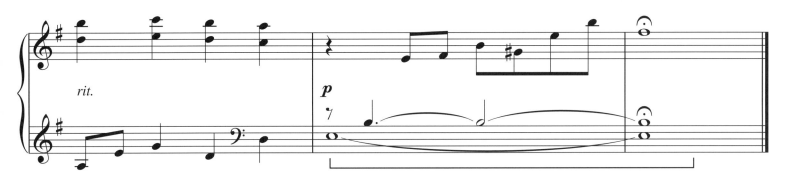

DO YOU HEAR WHAT I HEAR

Words and Music by NOEL REGNEY
and GLORIA SHAYNE

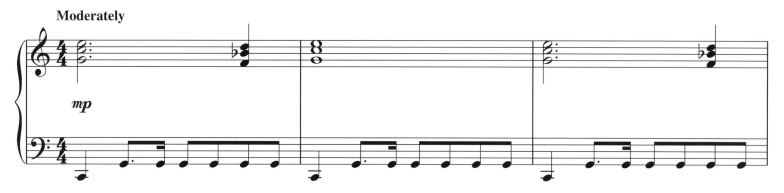

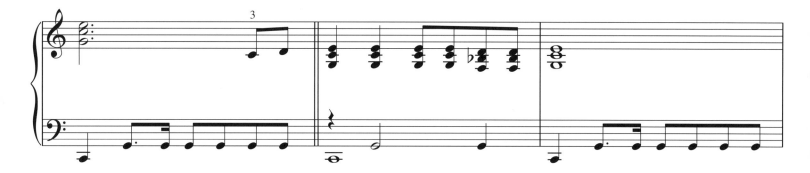

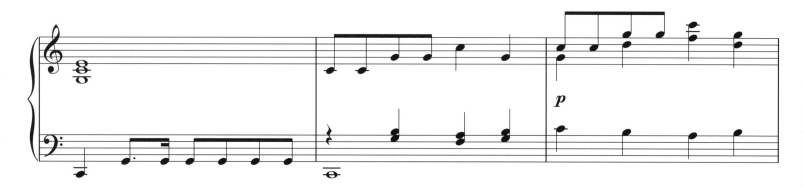

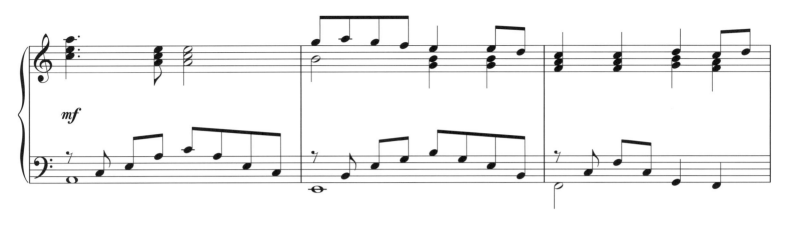

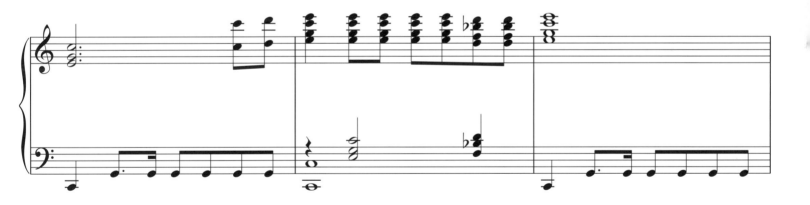

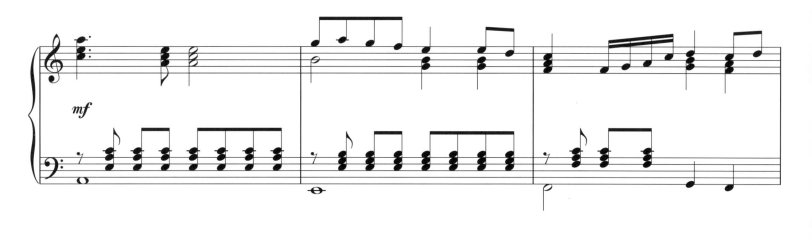

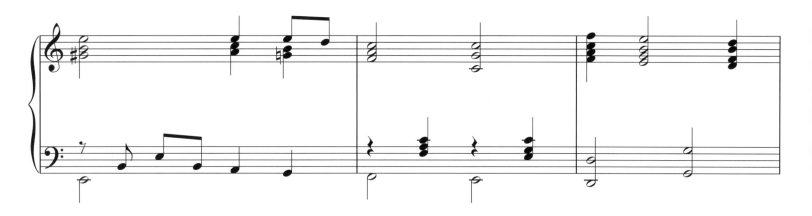

EMMANUEL

Words and Music by
MICHAEL W. SMITH

Moderately fast

add light pedal

To Coda

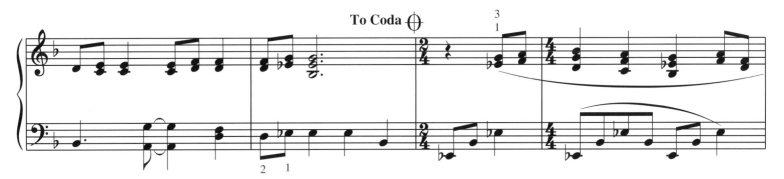

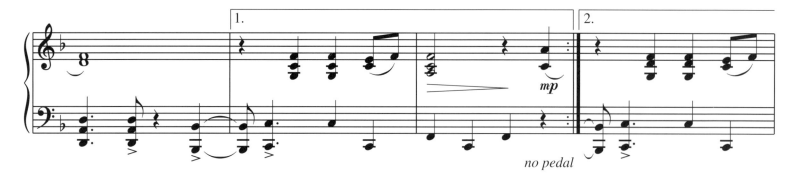

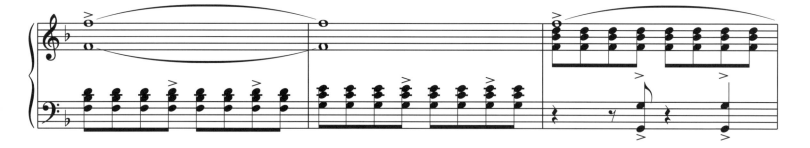

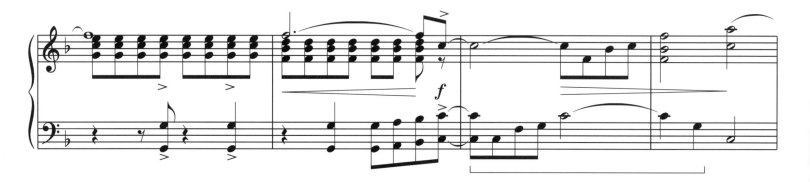

Repeat 3 times

no pedal

Repeat 2 times

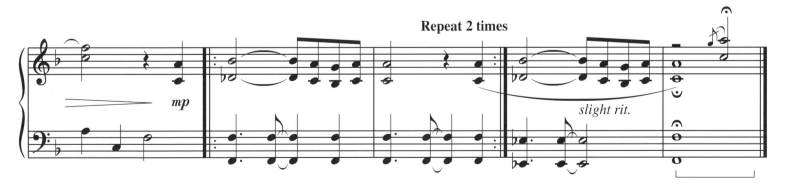

slight rit.

I WONDER AS I WANDER

By JOHN JACOB NILES

Slowly, with much expression

With pedal

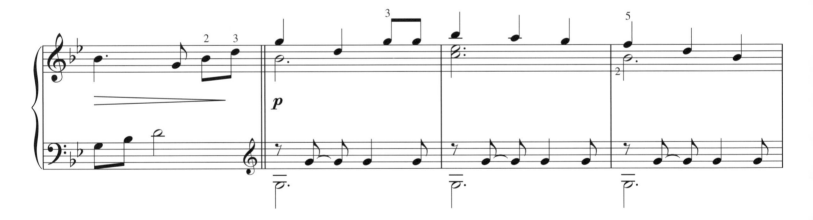

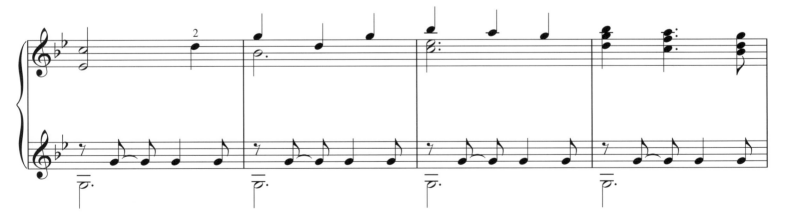

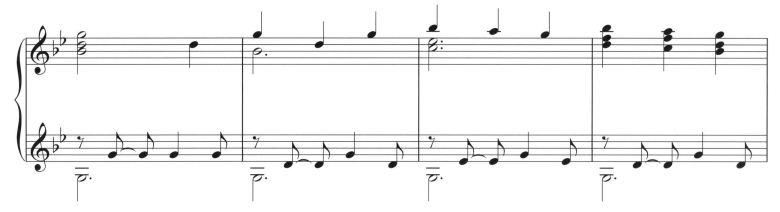

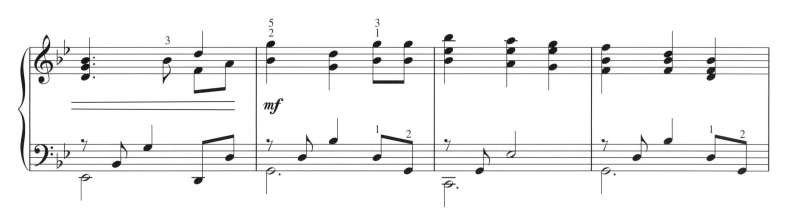

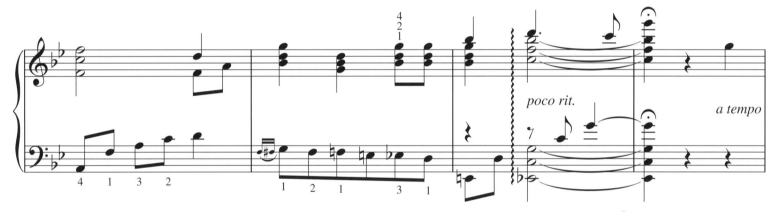

O HOLY NIGHT

French Words by PLACIDE CAPPEAU
English Words by JOHN S. DWIGHT
Music by ADOLPHE ADAM

Andante maestoso

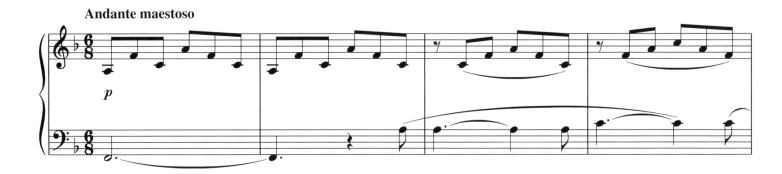

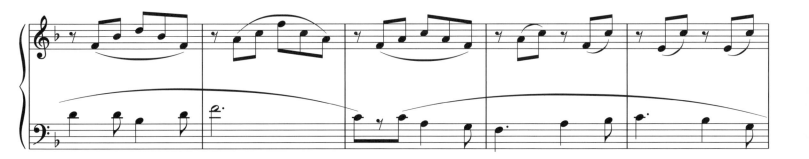

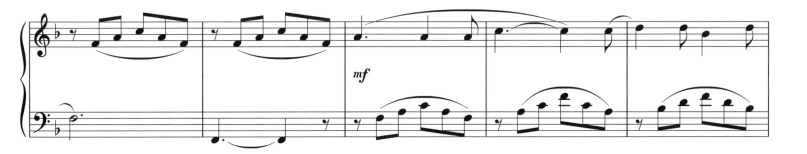

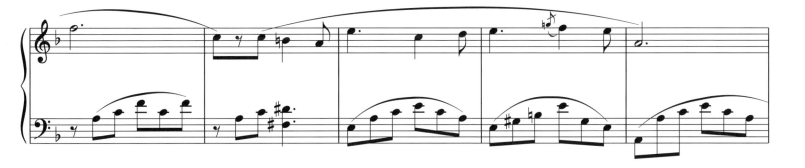

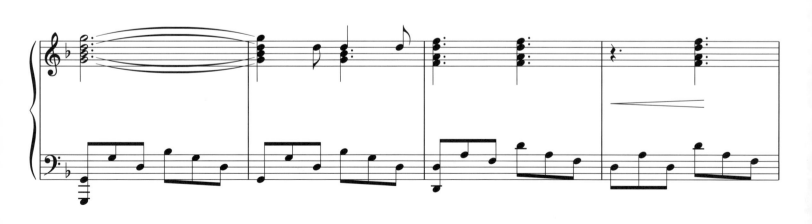

JOSEPH'S LULLABY

Words and Music by BART MILLARD
and BROWN BANNISTER

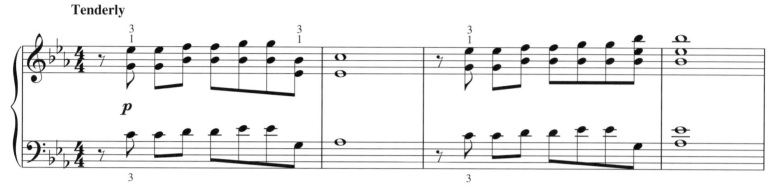

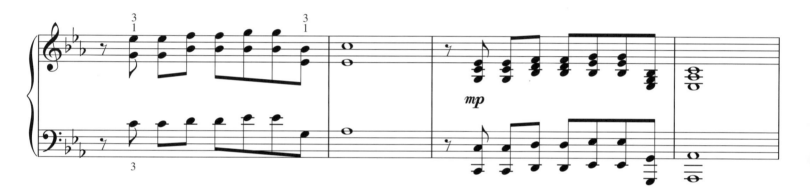

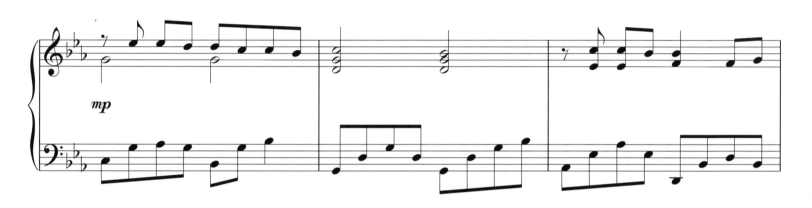

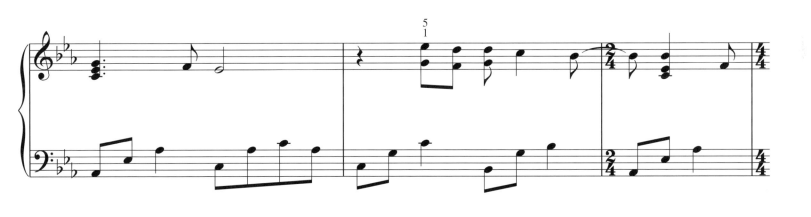

NOT THAT FAR FROM BETHLEHEM

Words and Music by JEFF BORDERS,
GAYLA BORDERS and LOWELL ALEXANDER

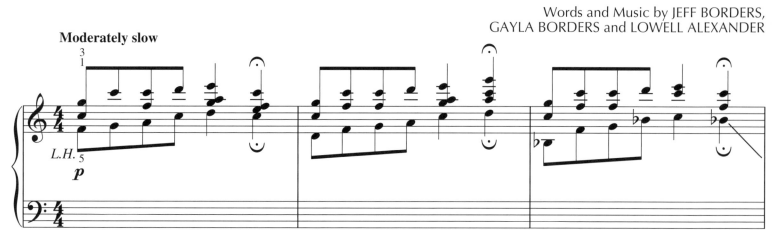

ROSE OF BETHLEHEM

Words and Music by
LOWELL ALEXANDER

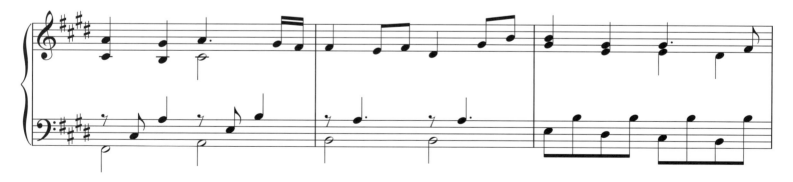

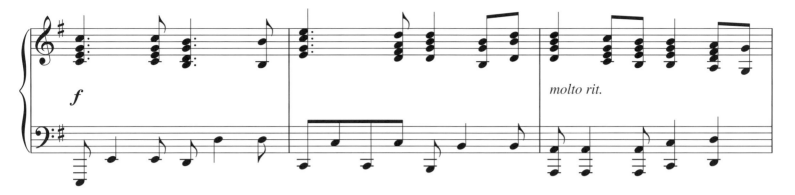

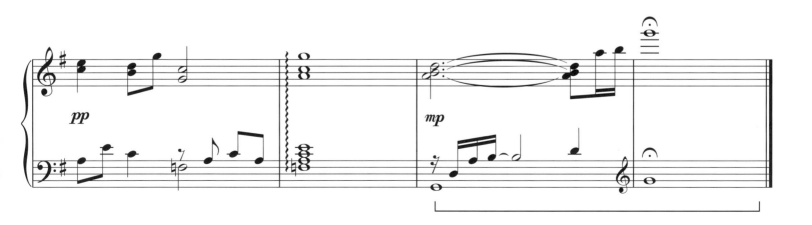

THIS LITTLE CHILD

Words and Music by
SCOTT WESLEY BROWN

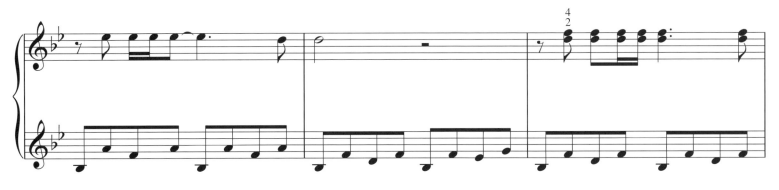

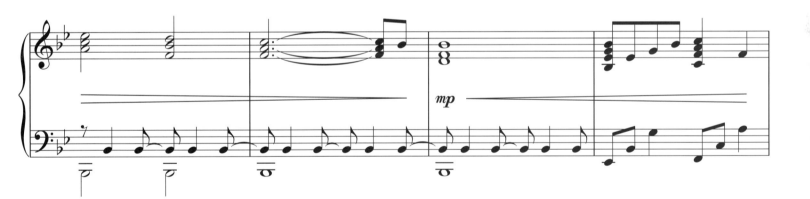

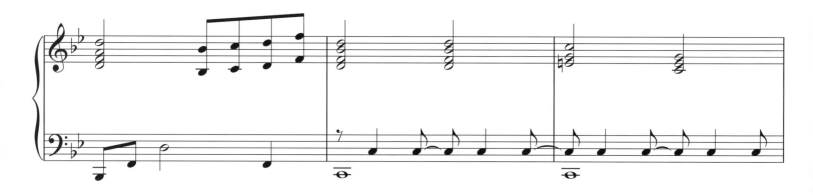

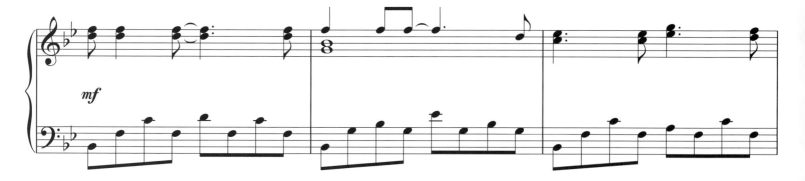

The Best Praise & Worship
Songbooks for Piano

Above All
THE PHILLIP KEVEREN SERIES
15 beautiful praise song piano solo arrangements, perfect for home or congregational use. Includes: Agnus Dei • Ancient of Days • Breathe • Draw Me Close • I Stand in Awe • I Want to Know You • More Love, More Power • Step by Step • We Fall Down • more.
00311024 Piano Solo..............................$11.95

The Best of Worship Together®
15 super-popular worship songs: Forever • He Reigns • Here I Am to Worship • Let Everything That Has Breath • and more.
00306635 P/V/G.......................................$9.95
00311143 Easy Piano $9.95

The Best Praise & Worship Songs Ever
80 all-time favorites: Breathe • Days of Elijah • Here I Am to Worship • I Could Sing of Your Love Forever • Open the Eyes of My Heart • Shout to the Lord • We Bow Down • dozens more.
00311057 P/V/G.....................................$19.95

The Best Praise & Worship Songs Ever – Easy Piano
Over 70 of the best P&W songs today, including: Awesome God • Blessed Be Your Name • Days of Elijah • Here I Am to Worship • Open the Eyes of My Heart • Shout to the Lord • We Fall Down • and more.
00311312 Easy Piano $17.95

Here I Am to Worship
30 top songs from such CCM stars as Rebecca St. James, Matt Redman, and others. Includes: Be Glorified • Enough • It Is You • Let My Words Be Few • Majesty • We Fall Down • You Alone • more.
00313270 P/V/G.....................................$14.95

Here I Am to Worship – For Kids
This great songbook lets the kids join in on 20 of the best modern worship songs, including: God of Wonders • He Is Exalted • The Heart of Worship • Song of Love • Wonderful Maker • and more.
00316098 Easy Piano $14.95

I Could Sing of Your Love Forever
THE PHILLIP KEVEREN SERIES
15 worship songs arranged for solo piano: Holy Ground • I Could Sing of Your Love Forever • I Love You Lord • In This Very Room • My Utmost for His Highest • The Potter's Hand • The Power of Your Love • Shout to the North • more.
00310905 Piano Solo..............................$12.95

Modern Worship
THE CHRISTIAN MUSICIAN SERIES
35 favorites of contemporary congregations, including: All Things Are Possible • Ancient of Days • The Heart of Worship • Holiness • I Could Sing of Your Love Forever • I Will Exalt Your Name • It Is You • We Fall Down • You Are My King (Amazing Love) • and more.
00310957 P/V/G..................................$14.95

Shout to the Lord!
THE PHILLIP KEVEREN SERIES
Moving arrangements of 14 praise song favorites, including: As the Deer • Great Is the Lord • More Precious than Silver • Oh Lord, You're Beautiful • Shine, Jesus, Shine • Shout to the Lord • Thy Word • and more.
00310699 Piano Solo..............................$12.95

Timeless Praise
THE PHILLIP KEVEREN SERIES
20 songs of worship arranged for easy piano by Phillip Keveren: El Shaddai • Give Thanks • How Beautiful • How Majestic Is Your Name • Oh Lord, You're Beautiful • People Need the Lord • Seek Ye First • There Is a Redeemer • Thy Word • and more.
00310712 Easy Piano $12.95

Worship Together® Favorites
All Over the World • Cry Out to Jesus • Empty Me • Everlasting God • Forever • Happy Day • Holy Is the Lord • How Deep the Father's Love for Us • How Great Is Our God • Indescribable • Join the Song • Ready for You • Wholly Yours • Yes You Have • You Never Let Go.
00313360 P/V/G.....................................$16.95

Worship Together® Favorites for Kids
Enough • Everlasting God • Forever • From the Inside Out • Holy Is the Lord • How Great Is Our God • Made to Worship • Mountain of God • Wholly Yours • The Wonderful Cross • Yes You Have • You Never Let Go.
00316109 Easy Piano $12.95

Worship Together® Platinum
22 of the best contemporary praise & worship songs: Be Glorified • Better Is One Day • Draw Me Close • Every Move I Make • Here I Am to Worship • I Could Sing of Your Love Forever • O Praise Him (All This for a King) • and more.
00306721 P/V/G.....................................$16.95

Worship – The Ultimate Collection
Matching folio with 24 top worship favorites, including: God of Wonders • He Reigns • Hungry (Falling on My Knees) • Lord, Reign in Me • Open the Eyes of My Heart • Yesterday, Today and Forever • and more.
00313337 P/V/G.....................................$17.95

FOR MORE INFORMATION, SEE YOUR LOCAL MUSIC DEALER, OR WRITE TO:

HAL•LEONARD®
CORPORATION
7777 W. BLUEMOUND RD. P.O. BOX 13819 MILWAUKEE, WI 53213

For complete song lists and to view our entire catalog of titles, please visit www.halleonard.com

Prices, contents, and availability subject to change without notice.

0407

CELEBRATE THE SEASON

with Christmas Songbooks for Piano from Hal Leonard

17 Super Christmas Hits

This book contains the most popular, most requested Christmas titles: The Christmas Song • Frosty the Snow Man • A Holly Jolly Christmas • Home for the Holidays • I'll Be Home for Christmas • It's Beginning to Look like Christmas • Jingle-Bell Rock • Let It Snow! Let It Snow! Let It Snow! • The Little Drummer Boy • Mister Santa • Sleigh Ride • We Need a Little Christmas • and more.
00240867 Big-Note Piano $9.95
00361053 Easy Piano $9.95

25 Top Christmas Songs

Includes: Blue Christmas • C-H-R-I-S-T-M-A-S • The Christmas Song • The Christmas Waltz • Do You Hear What I Hear • Have Yourself a Merry Little Christmas • Here Comes Santa Claus • Jingle-Bell Rock • Last Christmas • Pretty Paper • Silver Bells • and more.
00290064 Big-Note Piano $9.95
00490058 Easy Piano $10.95

Best Christmas Music

A giant collection of 62 Christmas favorites: Away in a Manger • Blue Christmas • The Chipmunk Song • The First Noel • Frosty the Snow Man • Grandma Got Run Over by a Reindeer • I Saw Mommy Kissing Santa Claus • Pretty Paper • Silver Bells • Wonderful Christmastime • more.
00310325 Big-Note Piano $14.95

The Best Christmas Songs Ever

A treasured collection of 70 songs: The Christmas Song • Frosty the Snow Man • Grandma Got Run Over by a Reindeer • Here Comes Santa Claus • A Holly Jolly Christmas • I'll Be Home for Christmas • Jingle-Bell Rock • Let It Snow! Let It Snow! Let It Snow! • Santa Claus Is Comin' to Town • more!
00364130 Easy Piano $18.95

Children's Christmas Songs

22 holiday favorites, including: Frosty the Snow Man • Jingle Bells • Jolly Old St. Nicholas • Rudolph, the Red-Nosed Reindeer • Up on the Housetop • and more!
00222547 Easy Piano $7.95

Christmas Pops

THE PHILLIP KEVEREN SERIES

18 holiday favorites: Because It's Christmas • Blue Christmas • Christmas Time Is Here • I'll Be Home for Christmas • Mary, Did You Know? • Rockin' Around the Christmas Tree • Silver Bells • Tennessee Christmas • more.
00311126 Easy Piano $12.95

Christmas Songs

12 songs, including: Caroling, Caroling • Christmas Time Is Here • Do You Hear What I Hear • Here Comes Santa Claus • It's Beginning to Look like Christmas • Little Saint Nick • Merry Christmas, Darling • Mistletoe and Holly • and more.
00311242 Easy Piano Solo..........................$8.95

Christmas Traditions

THE PHILLIP KEVEREN SERIES

20 beloved songs arranged for beginning soloists: Away in a Manger • Coventry Carol • Deck the Hall • God Rest Ye Merry, Gentlemen • Jingle Bells • Silent Night • We Three Kings of Orient Are • more.
00311117 Beginning Piano Solos...................$9.95

Greatest Christmas Hits

18 Christmas classics: Blue Christmas • Brazilian Sleigh Bells • The Christmas Song • Do You Hear What I Hear • Here Comes Santa Claus • I Saw Mommy Kissing Santa Claus • Silver Bells • This Christmas • more!
00311136 Big-Note Piano $9.95

Jazz Up Your Christmas

ARRANGED BY LEE EVANS

12 Christmas carols in a fresh perspective. Full arrangements may be played as a concert suite. Songs include: Deck the Hall • The First Noel • God Rest Ye Merry Gentlemen • The Holly and the Ivy • O Christmas Tree • What Child Is This? • and more.
00009040 Piano Solo $7.95

Jingle Jazz

THE PHILLIP KEVEREN SERIES

17 Christmas standards: Caroling, Caroling • The Christmas Song • I'll Be Home for Christmas • Jingle Bells • Merry Christmas, Darling • The Most Wonderful Time of the Year • Rudolph the Red-Nosed Reindeer • We Wish You a Merry Christmas • and more.
00310762 Piano Solo $12.95

100 Christmas Carols

Includes the Christmas classics: Angels We Have Heard on High • Bring a Torch, Jeannette Isabella • Dance of the Sugar Plum Fairy • The First Noel • Here We Come A-Wassailing • It Came upon the Midnight Clear • Joy to the World • Still, Still, Still • The Twelve Days of Christmas • We Three Kings of Orient Are • and more!
00311134 Easy Piano $14.95

The Nutcracker Suite

ARRANGED BY BILL BOYD

7 easy piano arrangements from Tchaikovsky's beloved ballet. Includes "Dance of the Sugar-Plum Fairy."
00110010 Easy Piano $8.95

The Ultimate Series: Christmas

The ultimate collection of Christmas classics includes 100 songs: Carol of the Bells • The Chipmunk Song • Christmas Time Is Here • Do You Hear What I Hear • The First Noel • Gesù Bambino • Happy Xmas (War Is Over) • Jesu, Joy of Man's Desiring • Silver and Gold • What Child Is This? • Wonderful Christmastime • and more.
00241003 Easy Piano $19.95

FOR MORE INFORMATION, SEE YOUR LOCAL MUSIC DEALER, OR WRITE TO:

HAL•LEONARD® CORPORATION

7777 W. BLUEMOUND RD. P.O. BOX 13819 MILWAUKEE, WI 53213

Complete songlists online at **www.halleonard.com**

Prices, contents and availability subject to change without notice.